CARRY'S

MAY
PATTERNS, PROJECTS & PLANS

by
Imogene Forte

Incentive Publications, Inc.
Nashville, Tennessee

Illustrated by Gayle Seaburg Harvey
Cover by Susan Eaddy
Edited by Sally Sharpe

ISBN 0-86530-140-9

Table of Contents

PREFACE

May – a merry month

MAY...

... A TIME of busy excitement — wrapping up a wonderful school year, preparing for summer activities and excursions, and enjoying the great outdoors.

... A TIME of exploring nature's treasures — gathering flowers to make May Day baskets, walking barefoot through the tall green grass, inspecting an abandoned bird's nest, and collecting insects and butterflies.

All of this and more is the "merriment" of May waiting to be brought into your "come alive" classroom. Watch students' smiles widen and their eyes brighten as your classroom says "the merry month of May is here" from the ceiling to the floor, from windows and doors, from work sheets and activity projects, from stories and books, and from an enthusiastic, "project planned" teacher.

This little book of MAY PATTERNS, PROJECTS & PLANS has been put together with tender loving care to help you be prepared to meet every one of the school days in May with special treats, learning projects and fun surprises that will make your students eager to participate in all phases of the daily schedule and look forward to the next day. Best of all, the patterns, projects and plans are ready for quick and easy use and require no elaborate materials and very little advance preparation.

For your convenience, the materials in this book have been organized around two major unit themes. Each of the patterns, projects and plans can be used independently of the unit plan, however, to be just as effective in classrooms in which teachers choose not to use a unit approach. All are planned to complement and enrich adopted curriculum schemes and to meet young children's interests and learning needs.

Major unit themes include:

- The Merry Month Of May
- Living Things

Each unit includes a major objective and things to do; poster/booklet cover, bulletin board or display; patterns; art and/or an assembly project; reproducible basic skills activities; and book, story and poem suggestions to make the literature connection.

Mini-units for the study of birds and insects are included in the "Living Things" unit and may be incorporated into the study of all living things or may be used individually. Other topics for which patterns, projects and plans have been provided include:

- Summer Birthdays
- Vacation/Travel

THE MERRY MONTH OF MAY

Major Objective:
Children will develop awareness of the sights, sounds, seasonal changes, special days and events that characterize the month of May.

Things To Do:
- Plan to spend as much time outside as possible. Plan field trips, excursions, walks, extra play time and time for going outside to "welcome the splendors" of the merry month of May! See pages 26 and 27 for a list of places to go!

- Reproduce a supply of field trip permission forms, name tags and follow-up sheets (see pages 28-30).

- Use the patterns in this book to make decorations for doors, windows, desks, etc.

- Reproduce the classroom helpers on page 20 and "have them ready" for use at appropriate times. Have on hand a supply of handy notes (pages 24 & 61) for this busy last month of school! The "Wrapping Up The School Year" form (page 77) can be used for children's drawings, booklet covers or notes to parents.

- Send the "letter to parents" (page 18) home to announce the month's activities and to ask for donations for your materials collection. Check your supplies to be sure that you are ready for the month!

To complete the activities in this book, you will need:

construction paper (assorted colors)	ribbon	plastic/glass jars
crayons & markers	broom	with lids
scissors	waste basket	dishwashing liquid
paste	Velcro strips	"bubble blowers"
adhesive & masking tape	stapler	(see pg. 31)
hole punch	pencils	milk cartons
blue & black or brown felt	water	index cards
ingredients for cupcake recipe	coat hangers	tempera paint
old magazines	yarn	paintbrushes
modeling clay	toothpicks	suet
short pipe cleaners	cotton	
string	cord	
birdseed	nail	

CELEBRATE MAY DAY!

Usher May into your classroom with a merry May Day celebration! Share the history and tradition associated with the celebration with the class.

> *May Day was first observed in England as a celebration of the arrival of spring. The custom of searching the woods and fields for wildflowers to fill May baskets has been preserved in folklore and village festivals over the years. (May baskets often are used as gifts for loved ones and sometimes are left on friends' and neighbors' doorsteps!) The high point of early May Day celebrations was the dance around the Maypole. A May Queen was selected to head the procession, and children carried flowers to honor the queen and her attendants. Celebrants wore festive clothing and decked themselves in flowers. The Maypole dance was followed by games and merrymaking!*

After the lively discussion that is sure to follow, help the class plan a May Day celebration. Have the children follow the directions below to make their own May Day flower crowns!

1. Cut a strip of colorful crepe paper for each child (two inches wide and long enough to wrap around the child's head and tie a bow).
2. Have the children use the patterns on page 11 to cut flowers from construction paper.
3. Help each child cut a hole in the center of each flower and slip the crepe paper strip through the flowers, pushing the flowers to the middle of the strip.
4. Instruct the children to paste the flowers in place.
5. Help the children fasten their crowns around their heads and tie bows to hold them in place.

FLOWERS FOR MAY DAY CROWNS

MAY DAY BASKET

What To Use:
1 qt. milk carton (one for each child)
construction paper (pastel colors)
scissors
paste
notes (page 24)
crayons & markers (optional)

What To Do:
1. Help each child cut off the top of a one-quart milk carton so that the carton is four inches tall. (This is the most difficult step. You may want to have parents help you with this project, if possible.)
2. Help each child cut out a strip of construction paper and paste it around the milk carton to cover the four sides.
3. Have each child cut a 2" x 14" strip of paper. Help the children paste the strips on their cartons to make handles.
4. Reproduce the flowers on pages 11 and 40 and have the children cut flowers out of construction paper to paste on their baskets. Or, have the children use crayons and markers to decorate their baskets.

Let the children fill their baskets with grass and flowers to make May Day surprises. Reproduce the notes on page 24 and help the children write special messages to tuck inside their May Day baskets.

Note: Half-pint milk cartons may be substituted for one-quart cartons if desired. Mini baskets are easier to make and fill. Use a half-gallon carton for a class participation basket to be delivered to the principal or director during a school parade or other event!

OUR VERY OWN MAYPOLE

Let the children help to make this simple Maypole for a class Maypole dance!

What To Use:
waste basket
books (or bricks, if you have them)
crepe paper (lots of rainbow colors)
scissors
masking tape
ribbons, flowers & other "scrap" items
broom

What To Do:
1. Stand a broom upright in a waste basket. Surround the broom with books or bricks to hold it in place.
2. Help each child cut a long streamer of crepe paper.
3. Allow each child to tape his or her streamer to the broom handle. (Begin at the top and work down the handle.)
4. After all of the streamers have been taped to the broom, add bows and flowers for decoration.

Now, let the real fun begin! Have each child hold his or her streamer and "dance" around the Maypole (clockwise), wrapping the streamers around the pole as the dance progresses.

Have the children sing "This Is The Way We Maypole Dance" (page 14) as they dance around the Maypole. Let the children carry rhythm band instruments or jingle bells tied to ribbons!

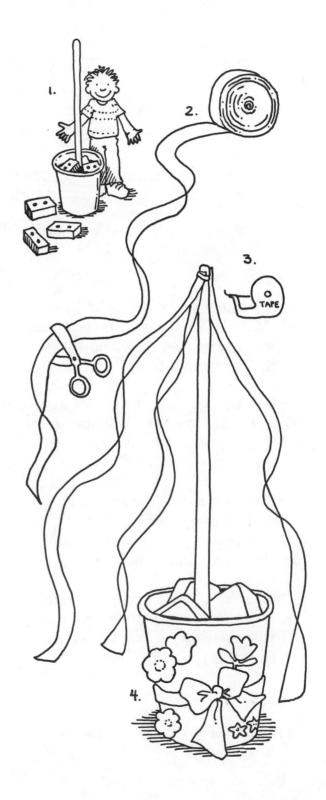

THIS IS THE WAY WE MAYPOLE DANCE

Sung to the tune of *The Mulberry Bush*.

This is the way we Maypole dance,
We Maypole dance, we Maypole dance,
This is the way we Maypole dance
In the merry month of May.

This is the way our streamers weave,
Our streamers weave, our streamers weave,
This is the way our streamers weave
In the merry month of May.

This is the way we move and sway,
Move and sway, move and sway,
This is the way we move and sway
In the merry month of May.

This is the way we sing our song,
Sing our song, sing our song,
This is the way we sing our song
In the merry month of May.

Repeat the first verse.

MAY ALPHABET

A ... April is over

B ... Blowing bubbles

C ... Catching butterflies

D ... Dancing around the Maypole

E ... Eating ice cream on warm afternoons

F ... Field trips and class excursions

G ... Getting ready for summer

H ... Happy May Day!

I ... Insects

J ... Jugs of lemonade for old-fashioned picnics

K ... Kisses and hugs for Mom on Mother's Day

L ... Learning about transportation

M ... May baskets to fill with flowers

N ... Noticing new flowers every day

O ... Outside fun, and learning, too!

P ... Picnics and parades

Q ... Queen of the Maypole

R ... Riding trikes and bikes after school

S ... Summer's almost here!

T ... Time to "watch a tree"

U ... Understanding the miracle of living things

V ... Vacation is on the way

W ... Wrapping up a wonderful year

X ... X-tra special time of year!

Y ... Yet another year is almost over

Z ... Zoo animals to "get to know"

MAY

Sunday	Monday	Tuesday	Wednesday	Thursday	Friday	Saturday

HOW TO USE THE MAY CALENDAR

Use the calendar to:

...find on what day of the week the first day of May falls

...count the number of days in May

...find the number on the calendar which represents May

...mark the birthdays of "May babies" in your room

...mark special days

- May Day (May 1)
- National Family Week (first week in May)
- Mother's Day (second Sunday in May)
- Memorial Day (May 30)
- etc.

CALENDAR ART

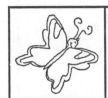 

Dear Parents,

May has arrived, and that means that the end of the school year is near. Our class has grown so much in so many ways this year, but we still have much to learn and do during the month of May!

In the days and weeks ahead we will be celebrating May Day, planning outdoor excursions, studying living things, and learning about transportation. Your child will be involved in various projects such as staging a classroom pet parade, making easy bird feeders, studying "insects in a jar," creating butterfly mobiles, and many other fun activities. Please read and discuss any work your child brings home to share with you, and help to encourage continued exploration and "learning curiosity" during the summer months.

You can help with our monthly projects by collecting and contributing empty milk cartons (be sure to wash them carefully with soap and water), birdseed, and plastic and glass jars with tight-fitting lids. Be sure to come by for a visit before the end of school!

Sincerely,

MAY MANAGEMENT CHART

CLASSROOM HELPERS

TEACHER'S HELPER

....

.... IS A GOOD WORKER!

MY TEACHER IS PROUD OF ME!

MAY

MAY DOORKNOB DECORATION

Color and cut out this doorknob decoration.
Hang it on your door to say that the merry month of May has arrived!

CUT OUT

HERE'S WHAT'S
HAPPENING
IN OUR CLASSROOM

Week of _____

MONDAY   _____

TUESDAY   _____

WEDNESDAY _____

THURSDAY _____

FRIDAY   _____

"THINGS TO DO" & "THANK-YOU" NOTES

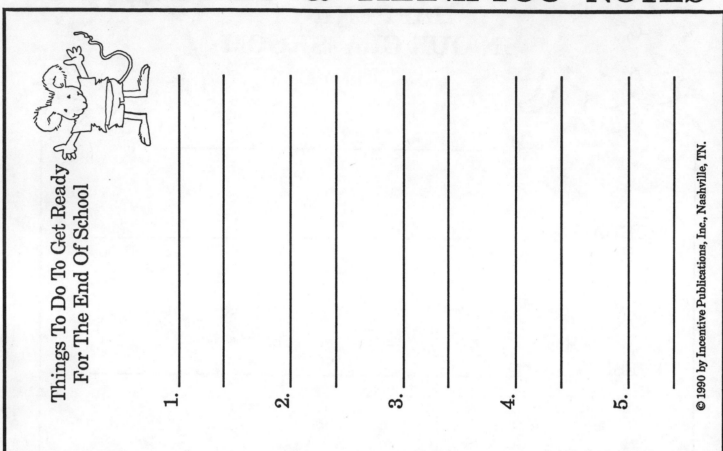

Things To Do To Get Ready For The End Of School

1.

2.

3.

4.

5.

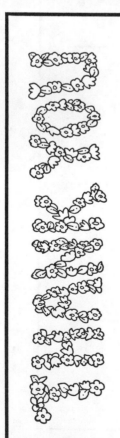

THANK YOU

PENCIL TOPPERS

"Top" your pencils with a butterfly or bee!

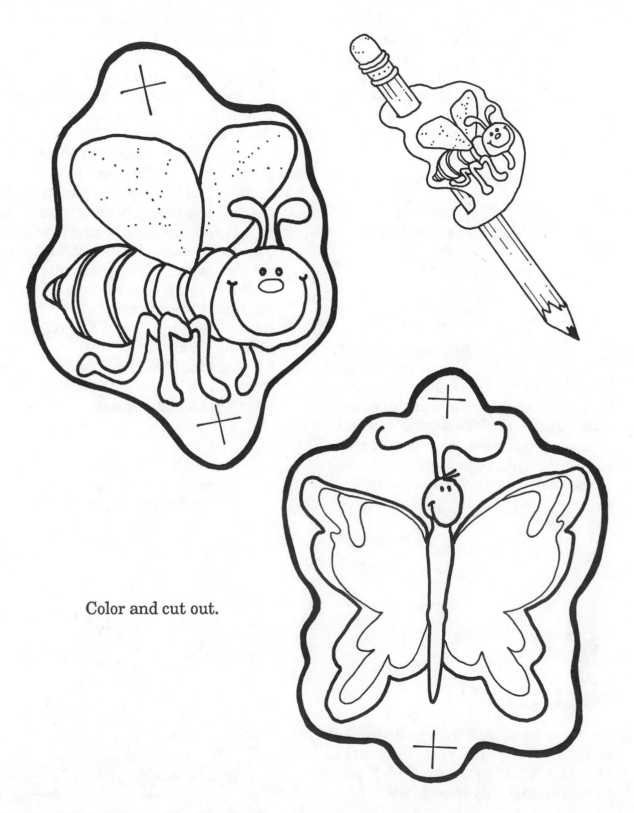

Color and cut out.

SUGGESTED FIELD TRIPS & EXCURSIONS

1. Take a walk around the school grounds or a nearby wooded lot to look for birds, birdhouses and bird nests. Make a list of the number and kinds of birds spotted and record the information on a chart for the science table. As a follow-up activity, read *A Pocketful Of Seasons* by Doris Van Liew Foster (see page 78).

2. Take a trip to a nearby creek or pond to study the plant and animal life. Plan to take animals and plants back to the classroom to include in a class vivarium. Take plastic or glass jars with tight-fitting lids to carry your treasure (make sure holes can be made in the jar lids).

3. Go fly a kite! Ask the children to bring kites to school on a designated Monday. Wait for a windy day and let the children fly their kites!

4. Plan outside art and science projects. Let the children blow bubbles using "homemade" bubble mix (see page 31)!

5. Watch a tree! Find a tree on or near the school grounds that you can watch during the month of May. Help the children tie a brightly colored ribbon around the tree to mark it as their tree "to watch." Take regular trips to the tree to observe the changes taking place as the days grow longer and warmer. The children might like to make up stories about funny things that could happen to the tree. Plan to spend at least one "story time" under the tree. Read *The Giving Tree* by Shel Silverstein (see page 78) and share some of his fun poetry from *Where The Sidewalk Ends* (see page 78) on another day.

6. Take a field trip to a farm, a zoo, a natural wildlife preserve, a nature museum and/or any other place in your community that affords the opportunity to study animals in their natural habitats. Place animal books on the reading table to reinforce concepts gained from these trips. Reproduce pages 46-51 in quantities to meet the needs of the class. Have the children color and cut out the animals to make "take home" booklets and/or posters for the bulletin board.

7. Plan a pet parade! Ask each child to bring a pet to school for a parade on the playground. (Carefully coordinate this with parents so that the animals are brought at the appointed time and stay only a brief time.) Let the children who do not have pets bring stuffed animals. If your situation is such that it is not practical to bring live animals to school, let all of the children bring stuffed animals for a "stuffed pet" parade!

8. Enjoy an old-fashioned picnic! Provide peanut butter and any of the following items: jam, bananas, raisins, sweet pickles, crackers and whole wheat bread. Allow the children to make creative choices and help the children prepare their own "sandwiches." Also provide apple slices, carrot sticks, animal crackers and pink lemonade. Head for a shady spot and let the picnic begin!

FIELD TRIP PERMISSION SLIP

 **WE ARE GOING ON A FIELD TRIP!**

When: _____

Where: _____

How: _____

Why: _____

Your child will need to bring:_____

_____

Please sign the permission slip below and have your child return it by

_____ .

_____

Teacher

- -

My child, _____ , has my permission to go on the field

trip to _____ on _____ .

I will be able to participate in this field trip if needed.   ____   ____

yes   no

I may be reached at this number: _____ .

_____

Parent

FIELD TRIP NAME TAGS

Hi!

MY NAME IS

. . . .

I AM ON A FIELD TRIP

HELLO!

I'M _____

MY CLASS IS
ON A
FIELD
TRIP

MY NAME IS

I'M ON A
FIELD TRIP WITH
MY CLASS.

Hi!

MY NAME IS

. . . .

I AM ON A
FIELD TRIP!

Name _____

OUR FIELD TRIP

Our class went to _____ .

This is what I saw.

BUBBLES TO BLOW

Bubble Mix

What To Use:
1 cup dishwashing liquid
1 gallon water
about 50 drops glycerin (optional)

What To Do:
1. Mix the dishwashing liquid and water.
2. Drop the glycerin into the water (to give strength to the bubbles).
3. Use a spoon or whisk to beat the mixture well.

Fill a basket with bubble makers:

    slotted spoons
    spatulas
    small strainers
    drinking straws
    canning jar rings
    potato mashers
    wire whisks
    spools
    combs
    etc.

Take the basket and the excited children outside on a sunny day. Allow the children to help make the bubble mix and to choose their own bubble makers. Then, let the children blow bubbles! As the children make bubbles of different sizes and shapes and compare the bubbles, they will use "lively language" and develop observation skills.

SANDY
SPRING SCENES

What To Use:
plastic containers (margarine, cottage
  cheese or ice cream containers)
liquid starch
fine sand
water
large spoon
tempera paint (red, white, blue,
  yellow, green)
crayons
paper

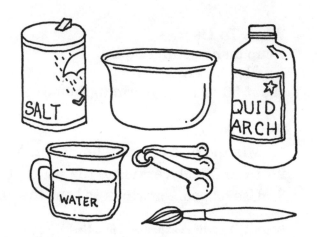

What To Do:

1. Mix salt, liquid starch and water together until the mixture is of an even
   spreading consistency. A good rule of thumb is to use one teaspoon each of
   liquid starch and water to two teaspoons of sand. The texture of the sand will
   affect the consistency, so you will need to experiment by adding water and
   liquid starch as needed. Fill several plastic containers with the mixture.

2. Help the children add tempera paint to each container to make red, pink,
   yellow, orange, blue, purple, green and white paint. (Note: This is a good
   science experience in color mixing!)

3. Ask the children to sketch simple nature scenes that may be observed in May
   (trees, a bird in a tree, butterflies, cloudy skies, etc.). Then have the children
   paint over their "outlines" with the various colors of sand paint to complete
   their "day in May" pictures.

LIVING THINGS

Major Objective:

Children will develop awareness of living things and their needs and will be able to distinguish between living and non-living things.

Things To Do:

- Create a flannel board to help the children classify living and non-living things. Cover half the board with blue felt and the other half with brown or black felt. Reproduce the banners on page 36 and color them with markers. Attach the "Living Things" banner to the blue half of the board and the "Non-Living Things" banner to the brown half. Reproduce pages 40-41, 45-51, 57-58, 65, and 68-69. Have the children color the pictures, cut them out, and paste them on squares of construction paper. Attach Velcro strips to the squares. Help the children place the pictures of living and non-living things on the correct sides of the board. (Additional pictures may be cut from magazines. The transportation patterns on page 75 may be used as pictures of non-living things.) Note: This activity also can be used as a bulletin board display.

- Reproduce two copies each of pages 45-49. Have the children color the animals, cut them out, and paste them on index cards. **1)** Let the children play a matching game. Each child is given several cards and then draws one card at a time from the deck, replacing one card from his or her hand at the bottom of the deck. The children are to match animal cards and "lay down" their matches as they are made. The first child to "lay down" all of his or her cards is the winner. **2)** Lead the children in a "name that animal" game. One child at a time draws a card from the deck, names the animal on the card and tells three things about the animal. When a child cannot do this correctly, he or she is out of the game. The last child in the game is the winner.

- Read Christina Rosetti's beautiful poem (page 71) and help the children learn it as a chant or choral reading. Have each child color and cut out a card and deliver it to a special person!

- Read *The Carrot Seed* by Ruth Krauss (see page 78). Share the pictures with the children as you read. Then ask the children to "dance" the story!

Complete mini-units for the study of insects and birds have been included in the living things unit.

Birds Mini-Unit Major Objective:
Children will gain knowledge of the characteristics and habits of birds and will learn that birds must have food, water and shelter.

- Ask the children to cut pictures of birds out of magazines and to paste the pictures on sheets of paper to make pages for a booklet. Help the children learn about the birds. Label each bird, make a cover, punch holes in the pages, and tie the pages together with yarn. Let each child take the book home for one day!

- Have the children inspect an abandoned bird's nest to see how it is made. Discuss how bird's nests are destroyed and how animals and people can help or harm birds. Place brightly colored yarn, straw and bits of cotton near low shrubs for the birds to use in making nests. Check daily to see what happens!

Insect Mini-Unit Major Objective:
Children will become acquainted with the physical characteristics and common habits of several insects and will observe insects in "daily life."

- Bring a harmless insect to class in a glass jar (punch air holes in the top). Have the children observe the insect during the day. At the end of the day, ask the children to tell what they observed. Record the observations on a chart for the science corner. Then, take the class outside to release the insect!

- Reproduce pages 67-68 for each child. Have the children color the posters. Help the children name the insects. Then discuss how each is helpful or harmful to human beings.

- Reproduce page 69 for each child. Cut and paste each bug on an index card. Have the children identify and classify the bugs as "helpful" or "harmful." The cards also may be used for matching, "acting out" or "name that bug" games.

Honey bunnies, bees and butterflies,

Ducks and chicks and little lambs-a-divey,

Oh for the merry month of May

When happy animals come out to play.

Name _____

Date _____

LIVING AND NON-LIVING THINGS BANNERS

Name _____

LIVING THINGS

All living things need air, sunlight and water.
Color the living things.
Make an X on 4 pictures of non-living things.

Recognizing living & non-living things
© 1990 by Incentive Publications, Inc., Nashville, TN.

Name _____

STUDY A PLANT

Plants are living things.
Most plants have roots, a stem, leaves and flowers or fruit.
Color the roots brown.
Color the stem and leaves green.
Color the flower yellow.

Recognizing plant parts
© 1990 by Incentive Publications, Inc., Nashville, TN.

Name _____

MISSING PLANT PARTS

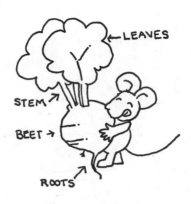

Draw the missing plant parts.
Color the plant.

FLOWERS

PLANTS

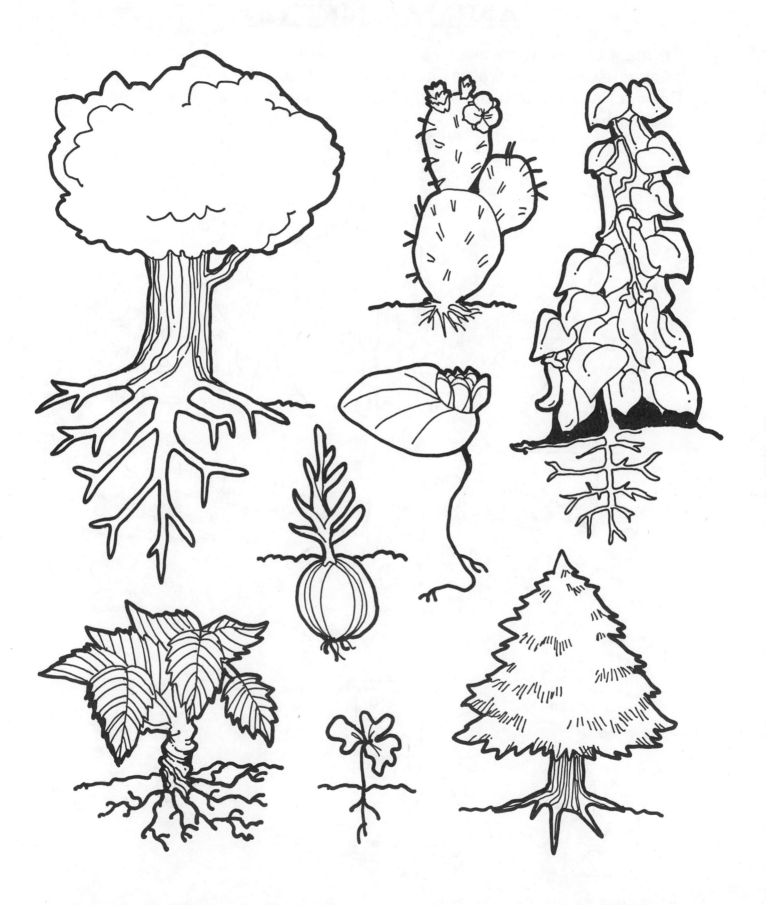

ANIMAL NEEDS

Animals are living things.

They must have air, water and food in order to grow.

Draw a line to match the food to the correct animal. Make an X on
the other foods.

Recognizing animal needs

© 1990 by Incentive Publications, Inc., Nashville, TN.

Name _____

ANIMAL PARADE

Color the farm animals brown.
Color the jungle animal black and yellow.
Color the forest animal red.

Identifying animals & their habitats
© 1990 by Incentive Publications, Inc., Nashville, TN.

MOTHERS AND BABIES

All of these animals are born alive.
Draw lines to match the mothers and their babies.

Matching animals & their young

PETS

Can you name these animals?
Color the picture of the one you would like to have for a pet.
Make up a story about you and your pet.

JUNGLE ANIMALS

FOREST ANIMALS

FARM ANIMALS

FARM ANIMALS

WATER LIFE

OCEAN LIFE

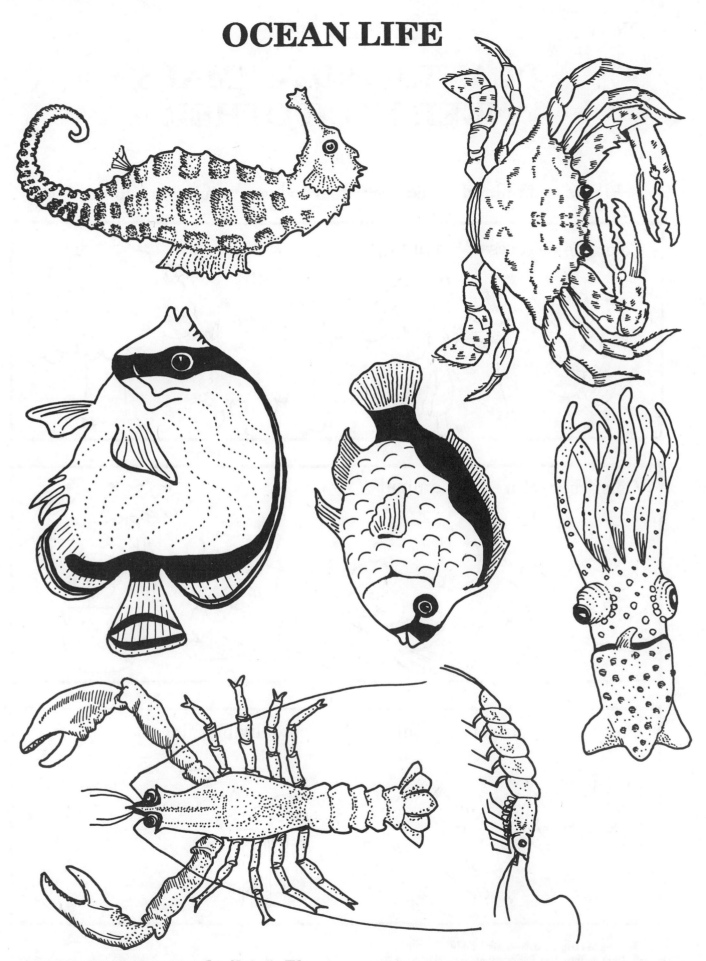

Name _____

PLANTS AND ANIMALS
NEED EACH OTHER

Plants and animals need each other to keep nature "in balance."

Color the pictures of 3 plants.

Color the pictures of 3 animals.

Color the picture of something that is not a living thing.

Recognizing plants & animals
© 1990 by Incentive Publications, Inc., Nashville, TN.

Name _____

A VERY IMPORTANT PERSON

You are a living thing.
Draw a picture of yourself doing something you really like to do.

I KNOW THE FIVE SENSES

Human beings use their five senses to enjoy life.
Cut and paste the labels in the correct spaces.

Eyes	Ears	Nose	Mouth	Hand

Recognizing the five senses

FIVE SENSES

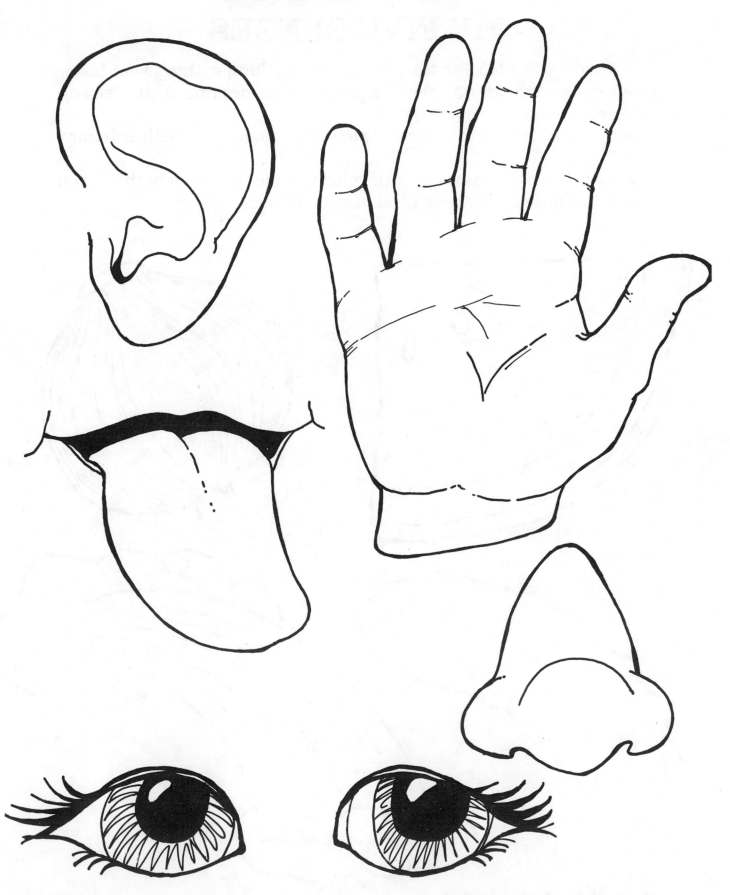

Name _____

MY FIVE SENSES

Use a red crayon to color the picture of something with a sweet taste.
Use a yellow crayon to color the picture of something with a strong smell.
Use a green crayon to color the picture of something with a bumpy feel.
Use rainbow colored crayons to color the picture of something you can see but cannot hear, smell, taste or touch.

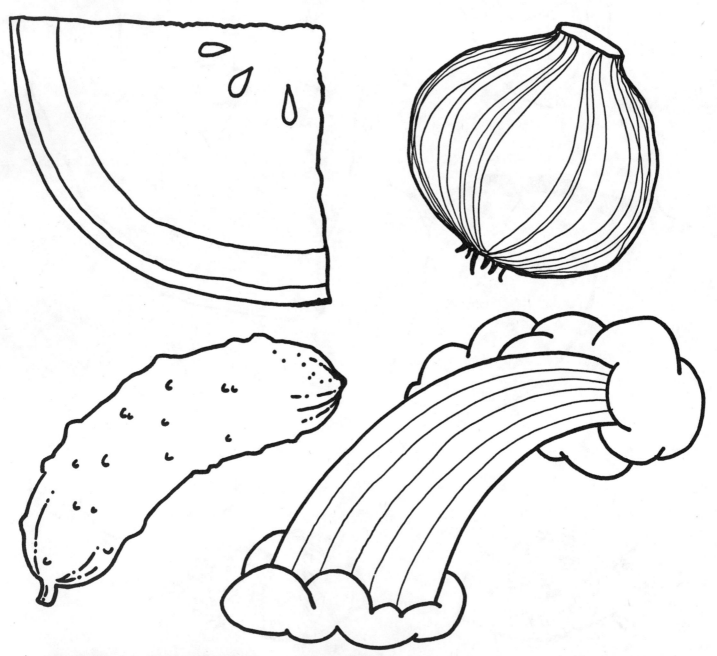

Identifying & understanding the five senses
© 1990 by Incentive Publications, Inc., Nashville, TN.

LIVING THINGS

NON-LIVING THINGS

Name _____

TWO BIRDS IN A NEST

Birds are hatched from eggs.
Mother birds build nests for their eggs.
The nest is the baby bird's first home.
Draw two baby birds for this nest.

Visualizing/creative expression
© 1990 by Incentive Publications, Inc., Nashville, TN.

HATCHED FROM EGGS

Color the animals that are hatched from eggs.
Make an X on the animals that are born alive.

Distinguishing animals that are hatched from eggs
© 1990 by Incentive Publications, Inc., Nashville, TN.

NOTES

Just A Note

To: _____

A Little Bird Told Me...

Name _____

BIRDS FLYING IN LINE WITH FEATHERS SO FINE

Finger Play	Movements
Five blue birds sitting in a tree,	Hold up 5 fingers of left hand.
The first bird said, "Look what I see."	Index finger points straight up.
The second bird said, "Five black birds in line."	Next finger points straight up.
The third bird said, "Their feathers are so fine."	Next finger points straight up.
The fourth bird said, "Quick, let's fly away!"	Left hand makes flying motion.
The fifth bird said, "No, let's all stay."	Hold up 5 fingers of left hand.
Then a black bird said, "Let's win!"	
"Join us, and we'll be ten."	Hold up all 10 fingers.
Well, all the birds flew together	Both hands make flying motion.
In all kinds of weather.	
Through the blue sky,	Flying motion "spreads out."
All ten would fly.	
Till one bright summer day,	
The blue birds in the tree did stay.	Hold up 5 fingers of left hand.
The black birds kept flying in line,	Right hand makes flying motion.
Leaving their new friends to pine.	
Once again they were five	Hold up 5 fingers of left hand.
and five!	Hold up 5 fingers up right hand.

1. How many birds were sitting in the tree? _____
2. How many birds flew away? _____
3. How many birds were there in all? _____

Counting
© 1990 by Incentive Publications, Inc., Nashville, TN.

INVITE A BIRD TO DINNER

This easy-to-make bird feeder can be an individualized art activity or a class project. Hang the bird feeder(s) near a classroom window — or let each child take home his or her very own bird feeder!

What To Use:
empty quart milk carton(s)
  (with pointed top)
cord
nail
suet
birdseed

What To Do:
1. Ask each child to bring an empty milk carton from home (remind the children to wash out the milk cartons with soap and water).
2. Help each child cut a "window" in one side of his or her milk carton.
3. Have each child glue or tape the top of the milk carton shut.
4. Help each child use a nail to make a hole in the top of the carton. Thread a piece of cord through the hole to make a loop for hanging.
5. Help the children roll pieces of suet in birdseed to place in their feeders.

Talk to the children about how birds need help getting food in winter. Then have the children help to roll pieces of suet in birdseed and tie brightly colored pieces of yarn around the "balls." Place the suet-seed balls on the window ledge or in trees near the window so that the children can observe the birds as they come to feed.

Name _____

FOR THE BIRDS

Color the pictures of things people can do to help the birds.
Circle one thing you and your family can do.

Recognizing ways to help birds
© 1990 by Incentive Publications, Inc., Nashville, TN.

BIRDS

INSTANT INSECTS

Review with the class the general characteristics of familiar insects. Remind the children that all insects have three main body parts and six legs.

What To Use:
short pipe cleaners
toothpicks
modeling clay or
    homemade play clay
tempera paint
paintbrushes

What To Do:
1. Give each child a ball of clay, six pipe cleaners and two or three toothpicks.
2. Instruct the children to "pinch off" pieces of clay and to form the body parts of an insect.
3. Help the children join their insect body parts with sections of toothpicks.
4. Direct the children to insert six pipe cleaners into their insects to make six legs.
5. Display the insects on a special table or windowsill.

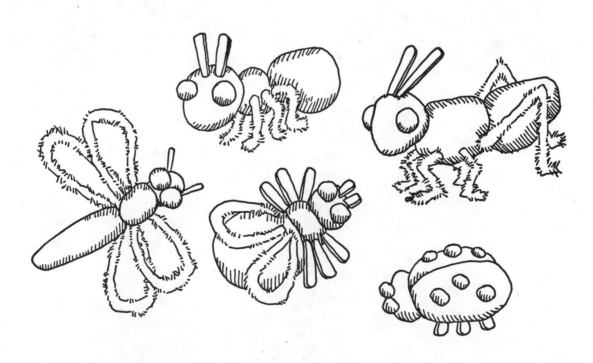

HARMFUL INSECTS

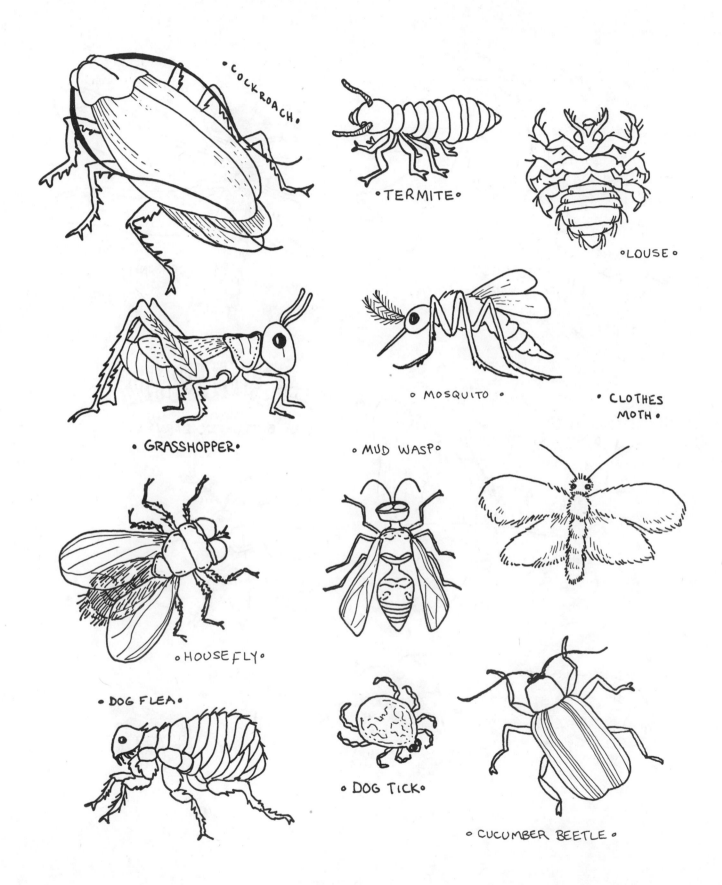

COCKROACH

TERMITE

LOUSE

GRASSHOPPER

MOSQUITO

CLOTHES MOTH

MUD WASP

HOUSEFLY

DOG FLEA

DOG TICK

CUCUMBER BEETLE

HELPFUL INSECTS

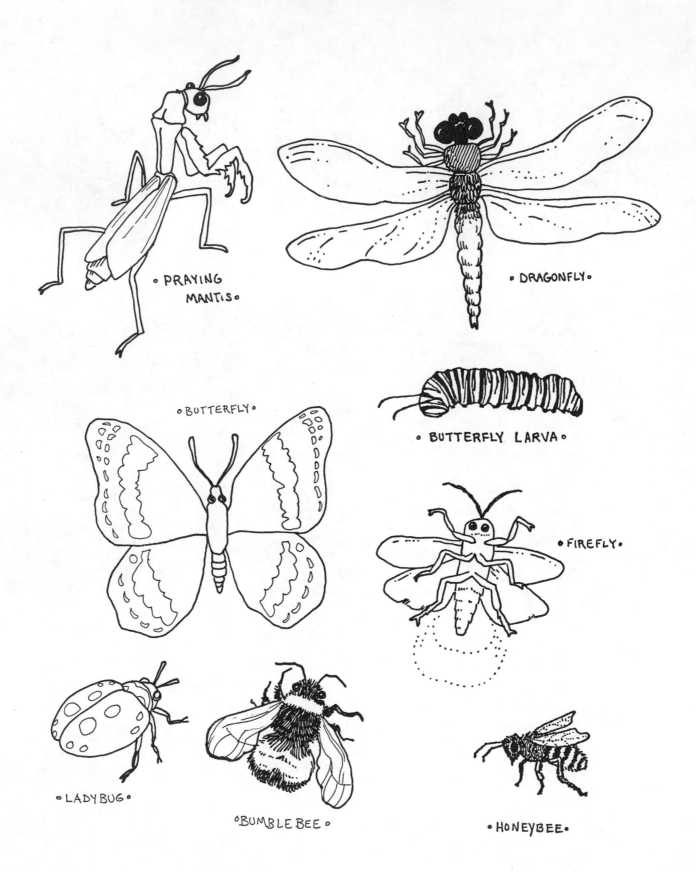

o PRAYING MANTIS o

o DRAGONFLY o

o BUTTERFLY o

o BUTTERFLY LARVA o

o FIREFLY o

o LADYBUG o

o BUMBLEBEE o

o HONEYBEE o

Name _____

BUG-A-BOO

Circle the helpful insects.
Make an X on the harmful insects.

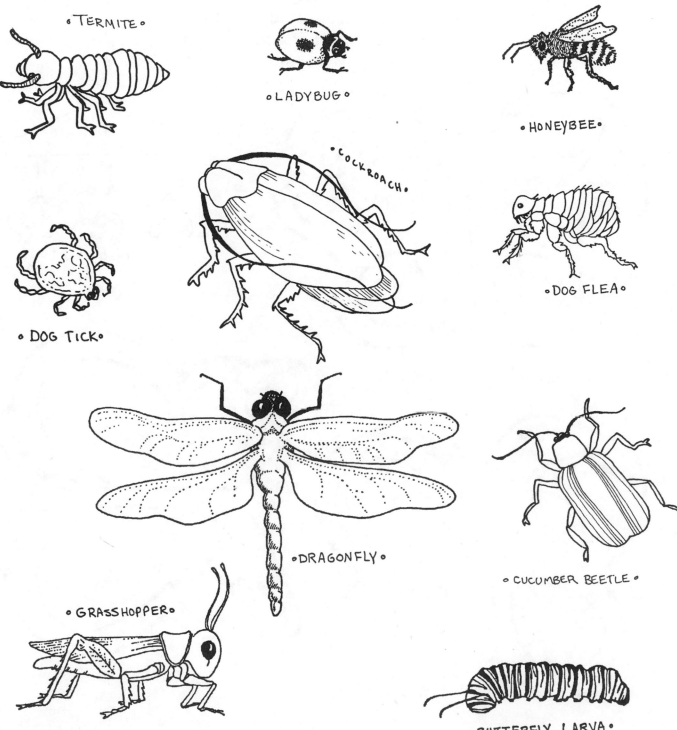

TERMITE

LADYBUG

HONEYBEE

COCKROACH

DOG TICK

DOG FLEA

DRAGONFLY

CUCUMBER BEETLE

GRASSHOPPER

BUTTERFLY LARVA

BUTTERFLY MOBILE

Make a butterfly mobile!
Here's how:

Color and cut out the butterflies.
Cut strands of string into several different lengths.
Punch a hole in each butterfly.
Tie one end of each string through a butterfly.
Tie the other end of each string to a coat hanger.

Following directions/constructing a mobile
© 1990 by Incentive Publications, Inc., Nashville, TN.

HURT NO
LIVING THING

Hurt no living thing
Ladybird nor butterfly nor moth with dusty wing
Nor cricket chirping cheerily
Nor grasshopper so light of leap
Nor dancing gnat
Nor beetle fat
Nor harmless worms that creep.

CHRISTINA ROSSETTI

FOLD

FOLD

FOLD

CUT OUT

CELEBRATE
SUMMER BIRTHDAYS

During this last month of school, celebrate "summer birthdays." Let one day be "Happy Birthday Day"!

1. Prepare a bulletin board display of a giant cake (cut from construction paper).
2. Make construction paper candles for each child who has a summer birthday. Write a child's name, age and birthday on each candle. Attach the candles to the cake.
3. Reproduce the notes on page 61 and use them as birthday cards for the children. (Example: A little bird told me you will be six on July 11. Have a happy day!)
4. Serve ice cream cone cupcakes and put a candle in each birthday child's cupcake. Sing "Happy Birthday" to each child separately!

Ice Cream Cone Cupcakes

What To Use:
1 box strawberry cake mix
ingredients called for on cake mix box
"flat-bottomed" ice cream cones
1 box powdered sugar

1 tsp. vanilla or strawberry
   flavoring
1/4 cup milk

What To Do:
1. Mix cake mix according to package directions.
2. Fill each cone with cake mix.
3. Place cones on cookie sheet and put them in preheated oven. (Follow cake mix directions for temperature and cooking time.)
4. Remove from oven and cool.
5. Mix powdered sugar and milk. Stir until mixture is of spreading consistency.
6. Add vanilla (or strawberry flavoring) and stir well.
7. Frost the cupcakes. (Optional: A few drops of red food coloring may be added to frosting if desired. A fresh strawberry may be placed atop each cupcake.)

VACATION IS ON THE WAY!

Lead a discussion about the many different ways families spend their summer vacation time. Be sure to include backyard and neighborhood fun, library and museum visits, fishing and picnicking in neighborhood parks and family reunions in order not to exclude children who will not take trips. This is the perfect time to help children develop understanding of the importance of transportation to daily life and the role it has played in the development of civilization.

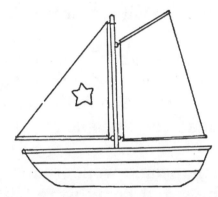

1. Read, or tell in your own words, the story on page 74. After discussing the story, involve the children in listing all of the ways they can think of to travel from one place to another. As the children supply words such as bus, train, car, airplane, ship, boat, etc., print the words on a chart.

2. After the children have exhausted their answers, review the words. Say something like this: "All of these means of transportation are dependent on some kind of power. Let's be scientists and see if we can name the sources of power." Through discussion, introduce the term "horsepower" and help the children to gain very simple, unrefined concepts related to the term. (Discuss engines, steam, wind, and horses. The depth of concept expectancy will have to be determined by the abilities and previous experiences of the children.)

3. On the following day, reproduce page 75 for each child. Ask the children to tell what kind of trip they would take on each means of transportation pictured. Then, ask each child to choose one vehicle he or she would like to use to take a summer trip. Allow each child to tell about the trip he or she would like to take. Have the children draw pictures of their "dream trips."

WAYS TO TRAVEL

Long, long ago, people had no way to travel other than by walking or riding on animals. This meant that people did not travel very far from where they were born. People had to get everything they needed for food, clothing and shelter from the land around them. They had no way of getting things from other villages. Life was hard.

Then, the wheel was invented. Wagons were built to move things from one place to another. Later, stones were moved and trees were cut down to make paths for the wagons. It wasn't long before roads were made and people really were going places!

Then, people wondered why they couldn't travel across water, too. So, ships and boats were built and greater distances were traveled. The next step was to travel through the air and, eventually, to travel into space.

Today we have so many ways to travel. Let's see how many we can name!

TRANSPORTATION VEHICLES

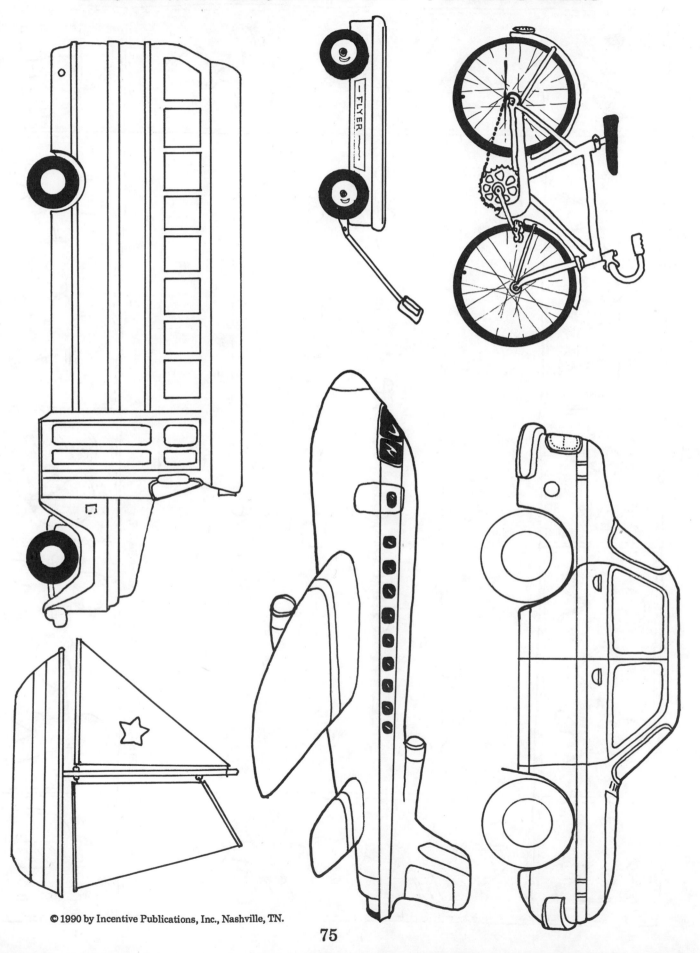

END-OF-YEAR CERTIFICATE

Dear _____,

I'm glad you were in my class this year. It was a great year.

Love, _____

_____
teacher

_____
date

We are wrapping up a wonderful year!

BIBLIOGRAPHY

Blossom Comes Home. James Herriot. St. Martin's Press.
When a farmer sadly sends his aged cow to be sold at the market, the cow escapes and returns home to find that the farmer will let her stay.

The Carrot Seed. Ruth Krauss. Harper & Row.
A determined little gardener plants a carrot seed and waits for the results.

How Many Bugs In A Box? David A. Carter. Little Simon.
A delightful pop-up book that allows children to "pull the tab" and count "four flat flies," "eight noodle bugs" and other fun bug groups.

Jungle Walk. Nancy Tafuri. Greenwillow Books.
A boy goes to sleep with his cat and dreams that his garden becomes a jungle, his cat becomes a tiger, and he has "meetings" with hippos, lions, zebras and other exotic animals. The boy and his cat wind up safely in their own bed.

The Little Engine That Could. Watty Piper. Platt and Munk Publishers.
Boys and girls are reminded to "try, try again" as they enjoy the story of a little blue engine that struggles to carry a load of animal toys and food to children on the other side of the mountain.

Nature Crafts. Imogene Forte. Incentive Publications, Inc.
Hands-on opportunities for children to explore, experiment and create with natural materials. Activities for indoors and outdoors ranging from puppets, periscopes and place mats to kaleidoscopes and cucumber soup.

A Pocketful Of Seasons. Doris Van Liew Foster. Lothrop, Lee & Shepard.
Something from each season is gathered by a young boy to be stored in his pocket.

Skates. Ezra Jack Keats. Franklin Watts, Inc.
A delightful picture book that needs no words to show how two friends almost give up their efforts to learn how to roller skate until the opportunity to help someone presents itself.

Spring Is A New Beginning. Joan Walsh Anglund. Harcourt Brace Jovanovich, Inc.
An exploration of tadpoles and other marvelous finds of the spring season.

Sunshine Makes The Seasons. Franklin Brantley. Thomas Y. Crowell.
A let's-read-and-find-out science book that traces seasonal changes through the year as determined by the sun shining on the earth.

Wings And Wheels. Cynthia Chapin. Albert Whitman & Co.
An explanation of various forms of transportation and the purpose of each vehicle.

Index